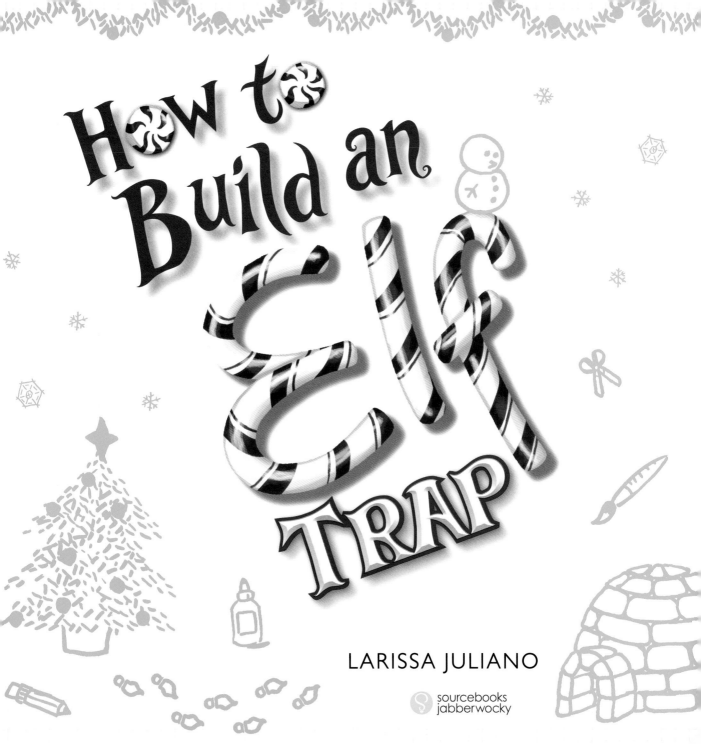

How to Build an Elf Trap

LARISSA JULIANO

sourcebooks
jabberwocky

Published by Sourcebooks Jabberwocky, Sourcebooks, Inc.
P.O. Box 4410, Naperville, Illinois 60567–4410
(630) 961-3900
Fax: (630) 961-2168
sourcebooks.com

Source of Production: 1010 Printing International, Kowloon, Hong Kong, China
Date of Production: June 2018
Run Number: 5012564

Printed and bound in China.
OGP 10 9 8 7 6 5 4 3 2 1

CONTENTS

NOTE TO PARENTS

More and more families have budding engineers and architects restless to create, manipulate, and produce something special. Whether it's cooking, constructing, or planning, this generation of children have inspired the STEAM movement—an approach to education that encourages discovery and inquiry through science, technology, engineering, arts, and mechanics. According to Engineering for Kids and the U.S. Department of Commerce, STEAM creates critical thinkers, enhances science literacy, and increases confidence and skill sets for future inventors. STEAM-based activities inspire playing, process, and piecing together elements. Endless research has proven that these experiences propel critical-thinking and problem-solving skills, as well as exposure to high-interest topics.

For parents, incorporating STEAM into our children's activities can be a daunting task as we try to keep up with the latest trends, endlessly poring over internet sites to find projects for the weekend that do not involve screen time. Luckily, experimenting with and building elf traps is a great STEAM challenge for families—it combines both holiday fun and hands-on learning! With this book, children will love creating the traps and experimenting with the additional Christmas activities, but they will also learn about how these projects work. Each trap and activity has a STEAM connection box that discusses the STEAM concepts. Parents and children can use these teaching points to generate questions, have thoughtful discussions, and then decide how to take scientific inquiries to the next level.

When it comes to STEAM-based projects, innovation is key. Discovery and experimentation are encouraged, so the trap directions, fun facts, and STEAM connections should be a stepping-stone and foundation to spark children's ideas and inquiries. This is the heart of these activities— stopping to critically think and innovate, engineer, or redesign something that kids come up with on their own. This can involve using different materials and tools or finding alternate methods and contraptions to lure in your sweet elf!

Technology can be incorporated into each and every trap by taking these STEAM connections and inquiries to inspire further research using digital and print resources at your local library. Having a variety of resources at their fingertips allows kids to pull information, check for accuracy, and report their findings. Using the tablet or computer (with adult supervision, of course) is just another way to enhance children's knowledge and add to their existing schema of how things work.

STEAM TALK

As parents of our budding scientists and engineers, we also play the role of STEAM facilitator. Try your best to take a step back and allow your children to problem-solve and analyze the directions, and make modifications as needed. Here are some great open-ended questions to engage in during the elf-trap construction process.

How does this trap work?

Why do you think this is the best material for that step?

Can you think of a better way to do this?

Can you look at the picture and try to build the trap without the directions?

Can you replace one of these materials with something else?

What can you add to this trap?

INTRODUCTION

Lots of us have heard about (and maybe have even tried) catching leprechauns, but have you thought about catching an elf? Legends of elves and other tiny mythical creatures have been around for centuries! Elves have been depicted in literature as early as the 1200s. They make a notable appearance in William Shakespeare's 1605 play, *A Midsummer Night's Dream*. Elves, fairies, and leprechauns are closely related in folklore, and as the generations have passed, elves have been depicted as playing different roles in nature and human interactions.

Christmas elves have the all-important job of assisting Santa in his travels and toy making, wish-list checking, and workshop managing. Known to be tiny creatures with pointy ears and magical powers, they also keep track of Santa's reindeer and have a watchful eye on little boys and girls, especially during the holiday season.

But elves aren't easy to catch—these Christmas fairies have a lot of tricks up their tiny red sleeves. Perfect family fun for snowy days and winter vacations, this book has twelve traps for you to try to catch one of Santa's helpers, along with other Christmas-themed activities to get you in the elf-catching mood. At the end of the book, there are a few planning pages to help you come up with your own trap and a set of stickers you can use to decorate these projects and lure in an elf! Note that all of these projects range in complexity but can be easily modified to add more dimension and innovation.

Keep an eye out for the STEAM connection boxes at the beginning of every activity, which take learning further. These sections look at how gravity works to knock over our trap cup, the role that acceleration plays in our chimney marble run, and the types of energy that factor into these ingenious designs.

So now it's time to grab some tinsel and candy canes and start planning for the perfect trap! Keep a lookout for tiny footprints and listen up for Christmas bells—elves will not be able to resist sneaking a peek at (and maybe being caught by) your clever contraptions.

NOTE ON MATERIALS

Materials will be listed on each project page, but many can be interchangeable depending on what you have on hand. Several traps require less common household materials, but most materials can easily be found at your local craft or home improvement store. Look at the materials list and plan ahead before you start construction!

- Some materials or tools may require the help of an adult. An asterisk (*) next to an item will denote this.
- Elf traps need extra Christmas sparkle. Check out your local dollar store for holiday-themed materials like felt trees, Santa stickers, miniature stockings, Christmas treat bags, garland, tinsel, and wrapping paper.
- Every trap requires some type of paint/markers/crayons, glue, tape, and construction paper, so always have those materials handy.
- Trim your traps with red, green, gold, and white accents (pipe cleaners, tinsel, or glitter glue) for extra elf appeal.
- Wrapping paper, wrapping paper, wrapping paper! Use wrapping paper to decorate boxes or other elements of your trap.
- Clay, putty, or play dough can all be used as a sticky base to affix signs or other trinkets you would like to stay put.
- Hot glue (requires <u>adult supervision</u>) works best for attaching most objects, but glue sticks or white craft glue can also be used.
- You can purchase colored craft sticks, or you can paint or color them yourself in holiday colors.
- Foam board and cardboard can be interchangeable, but foam is easier to cut.

Santa
Please Stop
Here!

THE ENCHANTING ELF DOOR

All elves welcome! This trap will trick even the savviest of Santa helpers—they'll get stuck before they realize it's a fake door!

DIFFICULTY

ELF APPEAL

STEAM CONNECTION

To catch our elf, this trap relies on *viscosity*—which is the thickness of a fluid. If a fluid has high viscosity (like honey or syrup), pouring it into a measuring cup may take several minutes. A fluid with low viscosity (like water) will take a matter of seconds. Experiment with different materials to create a high-viscosity, sticky substance for the welcome mat to catch our elf. Pour glues and syrups into individual cups and test the substances with craft sticks to see which stays put the longest!

MATERIALS

Aluminum foil
Craft wood or foam board, thin
Crafting knife*
Ruler
Gold paint
Paintbrush
Pipe cleaners
Hot glue gun*
White craft glue
Red candies

VISCOSITY WELCOME MAT EXPERIMENT (OPTIONAL)

Craft sticks
Small paper cups
Craft glue
School glue
Molasses, syrup, or honey
Shaving cream
Water
Putty

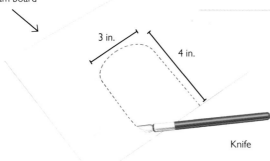

Foam board

3 in.

4 in.

Knife

1 Grab your ruler, and with <u>adult supervision</u>, use the crafting knife to cut out a 4 x 3 in. door from foam or a thin piece of crafter's wood.

To spice up your door, you can curve the top to give it an arch.

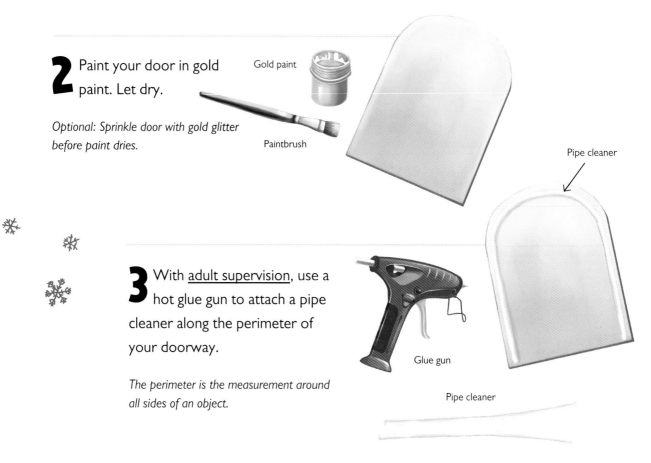

2 Paint your door in gold paint. Let dry.

Gold paint

Optional: Sprinkle door with gold glitter before paint dries.

Paintbrush

Pipe cleaner

3 With <u>adult supervision</u>, use a hot glue gun to attach a pipe cleaner along the perimeter of your doorway.

The perimeter is the measurement around all sides of an object.

Glue gun

Pipe cleaner

4 Create a window by shaping a pipe cleaner into a square, and with <u>adult supervision</u>, hot glue to the door.

Depending on how big you want the window, you might need to use multiple pipe cleaners.

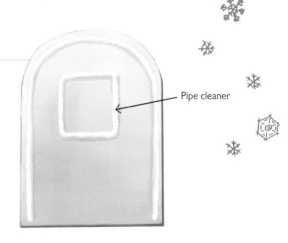

Pipe cleaner

Aluminum foil

5 Create a doorknob by taking a small piece of aluminum foil and rolling it into a pea-sized ball. With <u>adult supervision</u>, attach to the door with hot glue.

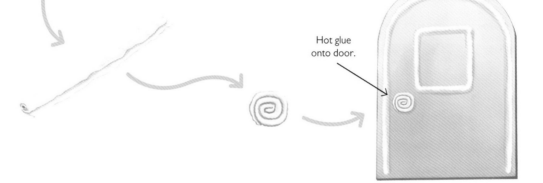

Hot glue onto door.

6 Make a doormat with a 3 x 2 in. piece of aluminum foil. Fold the sides of the foil up around the perimeter to create a little lip.

This is necessary to hold in the sticky substance in the next step!

3 in.

Aluminum foil

2 in.

DID YOU KNOW?

Elves can be tracked as far back as the thirteenth century in early Norse mythology! However, the idea of elves in Santa's workshop was only popularized in the mid-1800s.

7 Use the sticky mixture from the viscosity experiment or spread a layer of white glue onto the welcome mat and sprinkle with some red candies.

Glue

Red sprinkles

Very sticky mess

4

8 Place your door up against a wall with the welcome mat in front and check back to see if an elf gets caught in the glue mixture!

TEA LIGHT SNOWMEN

No snow needed to create these snowman magnets!

DIFFICULTY

ELF APPEAL

MATERIALS

Black felt or construction paper

Scissors*

LED tea lights

Hot glue gun*

Black puffy paint

Small heavy-duty magnets

STEAM CONNECTION

This project uses magnets to get the tea lights to stick to the refrigerator—but how *do* they stick? Magnets have a magnetic force that flows from the magnet's north and south poles, creating a magnetic field. This field causes two magnets to attract (come together) or repel (push away). Most refrigerators have steel doors with magnetic field lines that run through the metal, so when an object with a magnetic force is near, their opposite poles attract and the two objects stick together!

1 Use black felt or construction paper to cut out a top hat. With <u>adult supervision</u>, hot glue the hat to the tea light.

2 Use puffy paint to make dots for the snowman's eyes and smile.

3 With <u>adult supervision</u>, hot glue the magnet to the back of the tea light.

4 Switch on your snow-man's nose and display on a magnetic surface!

THE GINGERSNAP 400

Folktale fairies and fairytale favorites meet together to capture our pointy-hatted friend in this cleverly disguised gingerbread house!

DIFFICULTY

ELF APPEAL

MATERIALS

Large brown cardboard box

1 bag gumdrops

1 bag holiday candy

Red and white construction paper

1 wooden dowel

Paintbrush

Glue or tape

FOR SNOW PAINT

1 cup chilled shaving cream

½ cup craft glue

Glitter (optional)

Peppermint extract (optional)

STEAM CONNECTION

Without gravity, this trap wouldn't be possible! We use a stick to prop the box up and to get the trap in place for our elf, but gravity takes care of the rest. Gravity is the force that keeps the things around us on Earth—including people. It's because of gravitational force that after you jump, you come back down instead of floating away. Once the stick is knocked out from under the box, this same gravitational force pushes the box down to Earth and captures the elf inside!

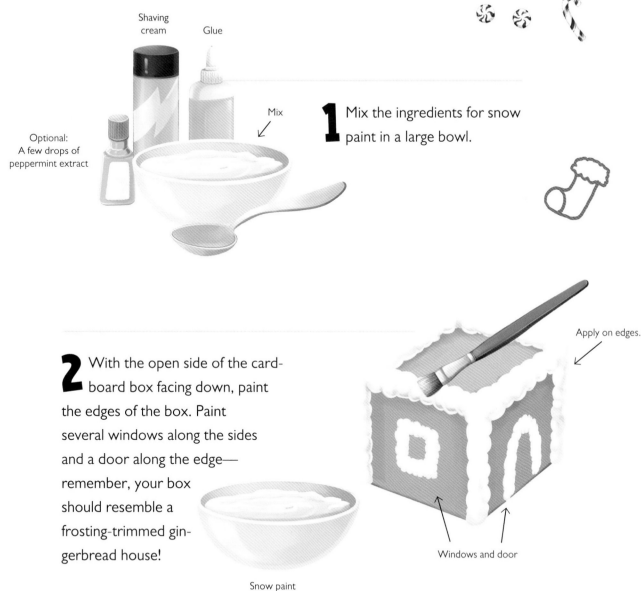

Shaving cream

Glue

Optional:
A few drops of
peppermint extract

Mix

1 Mix the ingredients for snow paint in a large bowl.

Apply on edges.

2 With the open side of the cardboard box facing down, paint the edges of the box. Paint several windows along the sides and a door along the edge—remember, your box should resemble a frosting-trimmed gingerbread house!

Windows and door

Snow paint

3 Add gumdrops on top of your sticky paint before it dries.

Gumdrops

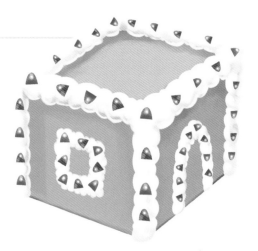

White strips with candy cane stripes

4 To create a candy cane pathway, take a sheet of white construction paper and cut five 11x1 in. strips. Color the strips with red stripes to make them look like candy cane sticks. Set one strip aside for step 5. Then, glue the other four strips to a piece of red construction paper.

Glue

Red paper

Candy cane pathway

DID YOU KNOW?

The world's largest gingerbread house was built in Bryan, Texas in 2013. It measured 60 ft. long by 42 ft. wide and 20 ft. tall. This house was not just for decoration—you could actually go inside and take pictures with Santa! It took 7,200 eggs, 7,200 pounds of flour, 3,000 pounds of sugar, 1,800 pounds of butter, and 22,000 candy pieces to create.

Wooden dowel

■ Now it's time to make your
◢ candy cane stick to prop up your
gingerbread house. Take your extra
candy cane strip from step 4 and
wrap it around your wooden dowel.
Use tape or glue to get the paper to
stay on the dowel.

6 Prop your candy cane
stick under your box.

■ ❯ Place your candy cane path
under the box and sprinkle
candy on top. Your hungry little elf
will not be able to resist a taste of
the "candy cane" stick. When he
goes to take a bite, the stick will
move and he'll be trapped in your
adorable gingerbread house!

Stick

Candies on
top of paper

GINGERBREAD PLAY DOUGH

Gingerbread cookies? Yes please! This play dough will engage our senses of touch, sight, and smell as we manipulate our spicy-smelling dough into various shapes and forms.

MATERIALS

2 cups all-purpose flour

¾ cup salt

2-4 tablespoons oil

½ cup water

1 tablespoon ground ginger

2 tablespoons ground cinnamon

Gingerbread man cookie cutter (optional)

Brown food coloring (a few drops)

DIFFICULTY

ELF APPEAL

STEAM CONNECTION

Play dough is a staple kinesthetic activity in all households! This recipe contains ingredients easily found in our pantries. What most affects the texture and consistency of the dough is the type of flour, the addition of cream of tartar, and the quantity of salt. The proteins in the flour (commonly known as gluten) combine with the heated water, resulting in a stretchy dough with loads of elasticity! Salt is a preservative that adds texture to the dough, and the oil keeps the dough moist and soft (not sticky). Who knew play dough could be so complex?

1 Add food coloring to the water and stir. Mix all of the dry ingredients together in a separate bowl.

2 Add the dry ingredients to the water. Mix. Add the oil and mix again.

3 Gently knead dough on a floured counter or cutting board.

Tip: If it is still sticky after forming and shaping, knead in one tablespoon of flour until it does not stick to your fingers.

4 Now it's time for fun! When you're done playing with the play dough, store it in an airtight container for several weeks of spicy-scented holiday fun!

NORTH POLE DINER

No elf can resist the thought of tasty treats on this holiday menu—
but they won't be able to get past the door!

DIFFICULTY

ELF APPEAL

MATERIALS

Shoebox or large boot box

Small utility knife*

Poster or foam board

Nontoxic acrylic paints

Paintbrush

Spool of ribbon (any color and/or width)

Craft sticks

Index cards for signs

Putty/clay

Dollhouse furniture or modeling clay (optional)

Ruler

STEAM CONNECTION

Mathematics plays a key role in decorating this trap. Measuring the ribbon for your window trimmings so it fits around the window and doorway adds an extra bit of authenticity! Use your ruler to determine if you want to measure in inches (the American measurement system) or centimeters (the metric system).

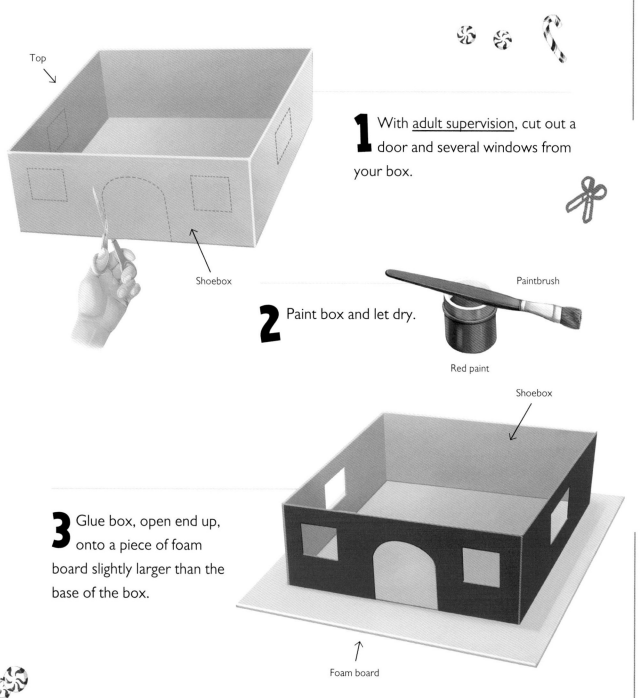

Top

Shoebox

1 With <u>adult supervision</u>, cut out a door and several windows from your box.

2 Paint box and let dry.

Paintbrush

Red paint

Shoebox

3 Glue box, open end up, onto a piece of foam board slightly larger than the base of the box.

Foam board

4 Take your ruler and ribbon and trim the windows and doors. Measure the top and sides of the eatery's openings and cut the ribbon accordingly.

Ribbon

COMING SOON!!

Toy furniture

5 Use dollhouse furniture (or make your own out of modeling clay) to create a restaurant scene with tables and chairs.

DID YOU KNOW?

If the conditions are right during a winter snowstorm, you might be able to hear thunder! This rare phenomenon, known as "thundersnow," occurs mostly near lakes and happens when warm air rises from the ground to create turbulent storm clouds. It can even be possible to see lightning through the snow!

6 Using your index cards and craft sticks, create two signs for your pop-up eatery. Stick the base of your sticks in putty or clay to ensure they stay put. These can go outside the doorway of your restaurant. Feel free to add more!

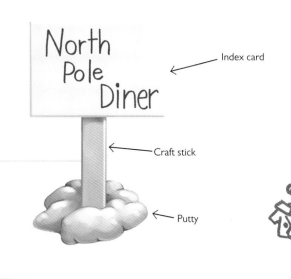

North Pole Diner

Index card

Craft stick

Putty

7 Take your putty and shape a small flat circle to stick inside the doorway. Your elf's nimble little feet will stick to this, and he will be trapped!

North Pole Diner

Fresh Food

Putty

REINDEER CUPCAKES

These delicious and moist carrot cupcakes will please the whole family…
as well provide a sweet treat for Santa and his trusty helpers.

DIFFICULTY

ELF APPEAL

INGREDIENTS AND MATERIALS

Makes about 24 cupcakes

4 large eggs

2 cups sugar

1 cup canola oil

2 cups all-purpose flour

2 teaspoons ground cinnamon

1 teaspoon baking powder

1 teaspoon ground allspice

½ teaspoon salt

Sprinkle of nutmeg (optional)

3 cups grated carrots

Large bowl and mixing spoon

Hand mixer*

Muffin tin

Cupcake liners (optional)

Cooking spray

FOR REINDEER DECORATION

Pretzel twists

1 container chocolate frosting

Brown and red chocolate candies for the nose

Candy googly eyes

STEAM CONNECTION

Did you know that chemical reactions play a big role in baking? When we add water to the baking powder, the two materials react to make carbon dioxide gas bubbles. It's important not to overmix or let the batter stand too long, or else the bubbles will start to deflate. Once the batter is in the oven, the heat causes the gas bubbles to expand and rise, creating our light and fluffy cupcakes!

1 Preheat the oven to 325°F.

2 Place cupcake liners in your muffin tin or grease pan.

3 In a bowl, use hand mixer on medium to beat eggs, sugar, and oil.

4 In a separate bowl, mix dry ingredients. Gradually add them to egg mixture.

Do not overmix—this will cause your cupcakes to become dense!

5 Stir in carrots.

6 Spoon the mixture into muffin pan, about halfway full. Bake for approximately 20–25 minutes (until a toothpick comes out clean). Let cool, then remove from tins.

7 To create a reindeer, spread frosting on a cupcake. Stick pretzels at the top of the cupcake to look like antlers. Add candy eyes and a nose, and you have your very own reindeer!

CANDY CANE LAND

Creativity and candy canes make this minty-smelling land the perfect attraction for an elf who likes to take long walks in the park!

DIFFICULTY

ELF APPEAL

MATERIALS

4 toilet-paper tubes

Green construction paper

Scissors*

Toothpicks

Craft glue

White paint

Paintbrush

24 x 36 in. foam board

4 dozen large candy canes

Gumdrops

Hot glue gun*

Tape

White index cards or construction paper

Putty

STEAM CONNECTION

In this trap, we are creating trap doors that act like levers to catch our elf. The toothpick through the middle of the door acts as the fulcrum—which is the spot where the lever is supported and can pivot. When the elf stands on either side of the toothpick, the force of the elf's weight on just that one side will cause the door to shift, dropping the elf inside!

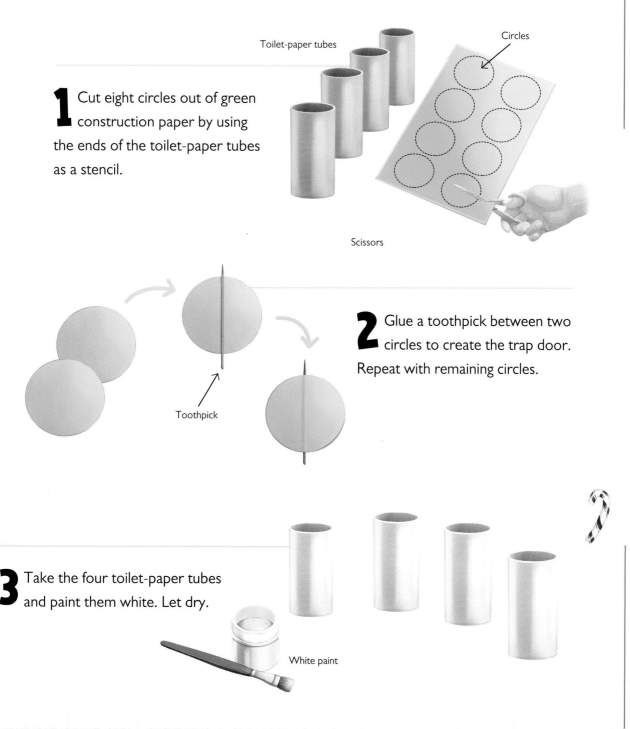

Toilet-paper tubes

Circles

1 Cut eight circles out of green construction paper by using the ends of the toilet-paper tubes as a stencil.

Scissors

2 Glue a toothpick between two circles to create the trap door. Repeat with remaining circles.

Toothpick

3 Take the four toilet-paper tubes and paint them white. Let dry.

White paint

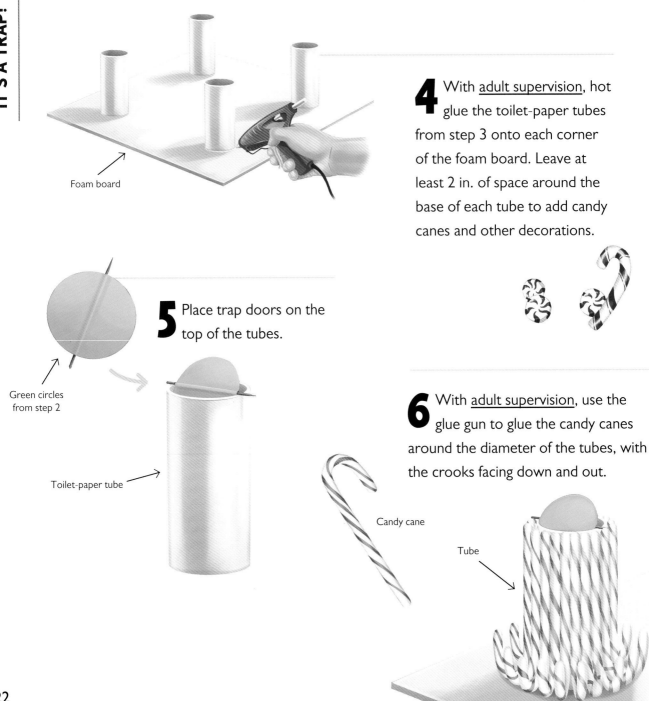

Foam board

4 With <u>adult supervision</u>, hot glue the toilet-paper tubes from step 3 onto each corner of the foam board. Leave at least 2 in. of space around the base of each tube to add candy canes and other decorations.

5 Place trap doors on the top of the tubes.

Green circles from step 2

Toilet-paper tube

6 With <u>adult supervision</u>, use the glue gun to glue the candy canes around the diameter of the tubes, with the crooks facing down and out.

Candy cane

Tube

Paper

Toothpick

Putty

7 Cut out trees from green construction paper and tape toothpicks across the backs to create trunks. Add a piece of putty on the bottom of each toothpick and spread them across your board to create a forest.

9 Using index cards, toothpicks, and putty, create four signs to place in front of each candy cane tube with enticing phrases to lure your elf inside! For example, "Free treats!" or "Candy cane tunnels below!"

8 Use the gumdrops to create a pathway on your foam board, and with <u>adult supervision</u>, use a hot glue gun to keep them in place.

Free treats

← Paper trees

Candy cane

Presents!

Elf Lounge

North Pole Playground

Gumdrop pathway along board

Four signs

CANDY CANE ICE CREAM IN A BAG

Jingle and shake away! You will need those twists and turns as you create a delicious icy treat…in a bag!

DIFFICULTY

ELF APPEAL

Serving size: Approximately one scoop of ice cream

MATERIALS

4 cups ice, cubed or crushed

1 cup half-and-half

6 tablespoons kosher salt

4 tablespoons sugar

½ teaspoon vanilla extract (optional)

2 pint-size resealable storage bags

1 gallon-size resealable storage bag

Crushed candy cane pieces

Optional: Toppings for ice cream (mini chocolate chips, sprinkles, nuts, etc.)

STEAM CONNECTION

Time for a delicious experiment! In this activity, we use salt to lower the freezing point of the ice, which is similar to the practice used in the winter to melt ice from roads and sidewalks. When the salt melts the ice in the resealable bags, we are creating the right temperature for the liquids to become cream. Shaking the bag mixes the cream so that it can freeze evenly—and it also adds air and fluff to the ice cream!

1 Add the half-and-half, sugar, and vanilla to one of the pint-size bags. Tightly seal and double bag inside the second pint-size bag to avoid leaks.

2 Put ice and salt in the large freezer bag. Then, place the pint-size bags into the large freezer bag. Make sure the freezer bag is well sealed!

Note: You will NOT be eating the contents of the large freezer bag!

3 Shake it! Wrap the freezer bag in a dish towel to avoid splatters and cold fingers. After five minutes, the cream mixture should get thicker. After eight minutes, you should have sweet, frothy ice cream all ready to eat!

4 Add in crushed candy cane pieces and other toppings and enjoy!

Tip: When you take out the bag with your ice cream, wipe it down carefully to get rid of the crunchy salt and ice condensation on the outside.

GARLAND FALLS

This trap is so colorful that no elf will spot the little trap door at the top!

DIFFICULTY

ELF APPEAL

MATERIALS

Empty coffee canister, with lid
Scissors*
Tape
1 sheet of tissue paper
2 ft. of garland
Pom-poms
Craft sticks
Green and red nontoxic acrylic paints
Paintbrush
Small utility knife*
Hot glue gun*
Candy cane
String

STEAM CONNECTION

Using your engineering skills is a must for this garland trap. Figuring out how to glue the craft sticks perpendicularly and fastening the stocking stuffer requires planning and experimentation.

Coffee can lid

Tissue paper

Tape

Tissue paper taped over cutout

1 With <u>adult supervision,</u> carefully cut a square or circle in the center of the coffee canister lid with the utility knife. Tape a piece of tissue paper over the hole and replace lid on can.

Garland

2 Wrap your garland around the can (but not the lid) and tape both ends securely so the garland stays put.

Tape both ends.

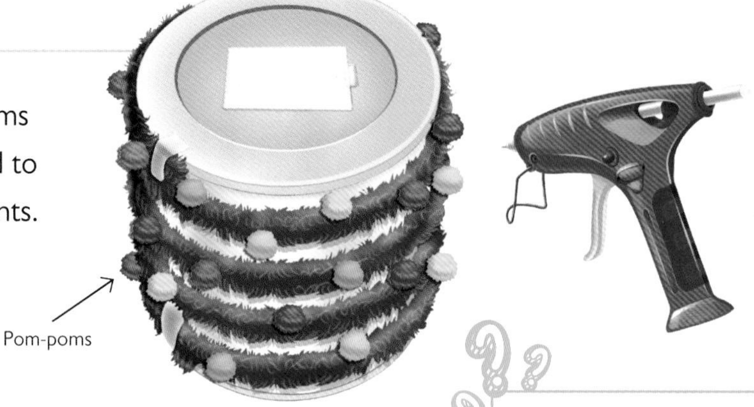

3 Glue pom-poms on the garland to resemble ornaments.

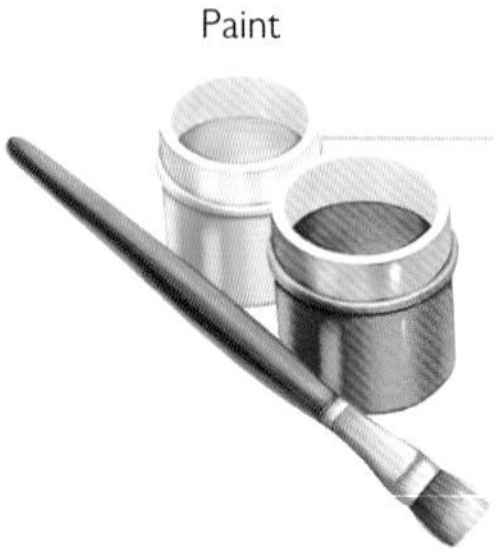

Pom-poms

Paint

4 Paint your craft sticks red and green. Let dry.

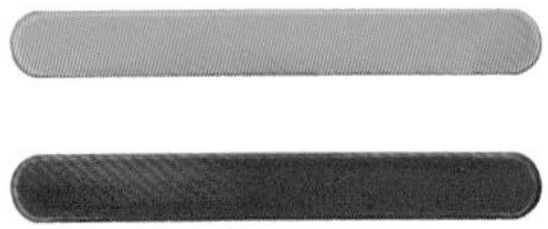

Craft sticks

DID YOU KNOW?

In 2007, the Children's Society in London made the world's largest Christmas stocking! It was 106 ft. long and 49 ft. wide. This stocking held almost 1,000 presents and was as heavy as five reindeer!

5 Use the craft sticks to create a ladder. With <u>adult supervision,</u> hot glue the craft sticks together and lean the top of the ladder up against the coffee can.

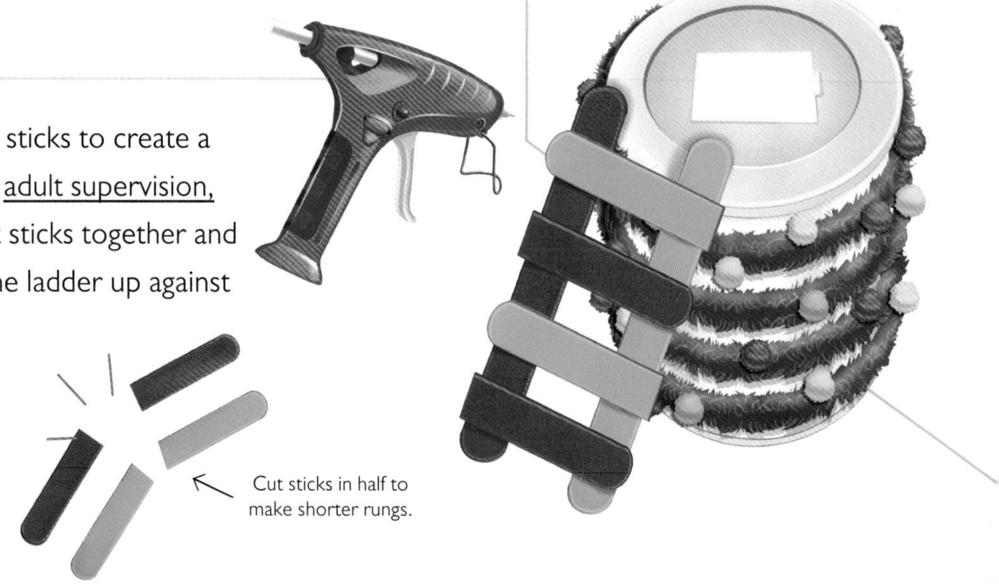

Cut sticks in half to make shorter rungs.

Craft sticks

Glue

6 With <u>adult supervision</u>, glue a craft stick under the garland with the top sticking up several inches out of the garland. Glue a second stick perpendicularly at the top of the first stick. The second stick should be above the tissue paper trap door.

7 Hang a candy cane over the trap door— your elf won't be able to resist diving after this yummy treat!

Candy cane

THE ELF IGLOO

Create a papier-mâché igloo for your elf to snuggle in during those chilly Arctic nights.

DIFFICULTY

ELF APPEAL

MATERIALS

Vellum paper

1 4oz. bottle all-purpose glue

¼ cup water

2 bowls that can get messy (at least one medium size)

Balloon

Tape

Marker

Hot glue gun*

Large oatmeal canister covered in plastic wrap

(optional)

STEAM CONNECTION

Get ready for fun papier-mâché in this activity! This art technique has been around for centuries—in ancient China, papier-mâché was used to create helmets and armor, and Japanese and Persian cultures used this technique to make masks. Combining water and glue creates the special paste that is used to soak the paper strips and create a hard shell-like material.

1 Tear vellum paper into strips of various lengths.

2 Mix the entire contents of the bottle of glue with water in a bowl and set aside.

3 Blow up a balloon and place it in the medium-size bowl with tape to stabilize. Use a marker to carefully outline the door and the bottom of the igloo on the balloon.

4 Dip vellum paper strips into glue mixture. Submerge strips completely, then wipe off excess glue. Cover surface of balloon above bowl with paper strips in a crisscross manner, leaving the door clear. Let dry until hard.

Note: For a quicker drying time, create only one layer of paper strips over the balloon. Some of the strips can overlap.

5 Optional doorway: Lay oatmeal canister on its side and use as a cast for the doorway by layering glue paper strips on top.

Make the doorway as long as you want—covering the whole length of the canister's side will create a longer doorway.

6 Carefully deflate balloon and slowly remove from the inside of the igloo.

Balloon might stick to the igloo, so remove it carefully to avoid damage.

7 Optional doorway: With <u>adult supervision</u>, use hot glue gun to attach the doorway to the igloo.

Papier-mâché strip for doorway

Oatmeal canister

THE ELF SNATCHER 500

Any elf will be tricked by this drawbridge trap disguised as a beautifully wrapped present!

DIFFICULTY

ELF APPEAL

MATERIALS

Small square box

Scissors or craft knife*

Wrapping paper

Tape

Screwdriver

Spool of ribbon, thin

Foam board

Self-adhesive magnet strip (optional)

STEAM CONNECTION

A drawbridge is a heavy movable bridge that could be raised during attacks for protection. Castle defenders could lift one end of the bridge into the air by winching up chains or ropes and sealing the drawbridge against the side of the castle like a huge door. Drawbridges were very heavy, so there was usually a counterweight (a really heavy object) to help pull up the bridge. In this trap, the gold coin acts as both the counterweight and the bait for our elf! Once he pulls on the coin, it will apply force to the drawbridge (and ribbons), which will close shut. The magnet adhesive lining the edges will apply extra pressure to the door to ensure it stays closed.

1 Cut out a 3 x 2 in. door on the base of your box, leaving the bottom part attached like a hinge so it opens and closes vertically—this will be your drawbridge.

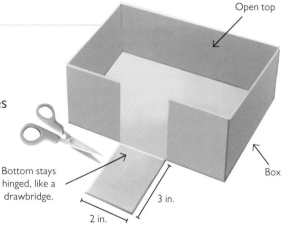

Open top

Box

Bottom stays hinged, like a drawbridge.

2 in.

3 in.

Top of box

Wrap all around.

2 Wrap the top and bottom of your box with wrapping paper and secure with tape. Make sure to cut and fold the paper carefully around the door!

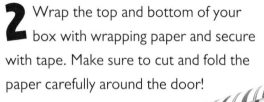

Wrapping paper

Tape

3 With <u>adult supervision</u>, use a screwdriver to poke one hole each through the top two corners of the drawbridge. Poke another hole in the center of the back of the box— this should be the opposite side of the door.

Poke two holes.

Back of box

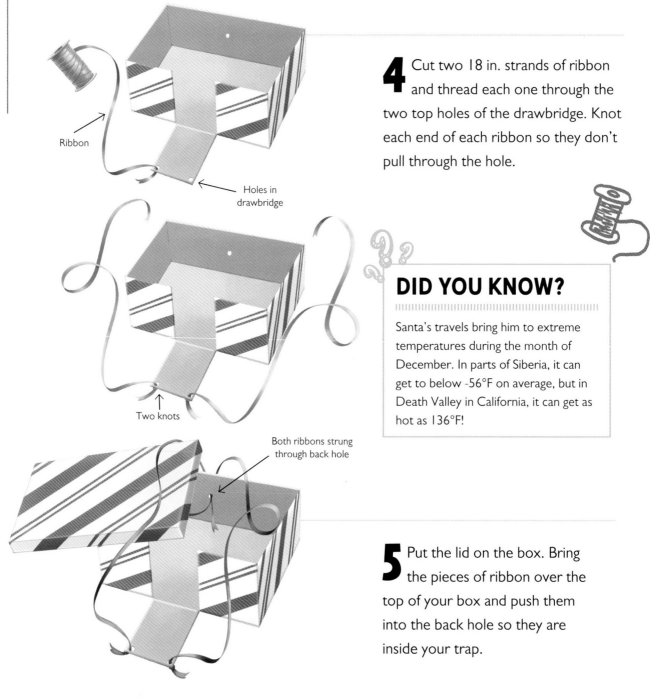

Ribbon

Holes in drawbridge

Two knots

Both ribbons strung through back hole

4 Cut two 18 in. strands of ribbon and thread each one through the two top holes of the drawbridge. Knot each end of each ribbon so they don't pull through the hole.

DID YOU KNOW?

Santa's travels bring him to extreme temperatures during the month of December. In parts of Siberia, it can get to below -56°F on average, but in Death Valley in California, it can get as hot as 136°F!

5 Put the lid on the box. Bring the pieces of ribbon over the top of your box and push them into the back hole so they are inside your trap.

6 Create a gold coin by cutting a circle out of foam board, approximately 2 in. in diameter, and paint gold. Let dry.

7 With <u>adult supervision,</u> punch two holes through the center of the coin, side by side.

Poke two holes.

Foam board

Paint

8 Take the two dangling ribbon ends from step 5. Thread and knot them through the holes in the gold coin. Once your elf pulls this coin down—snap! The ribbon will pull the door shut!

Optional: Take four pieces of self-adhesive magnet and line the door and entryway to ensure that it will stay closed.

Self-adhesive magnet

Tip: Add magnets to ensure door stays shut!

The elf pulls the coin down and snaps the door shut!

SUGARPLUM CATAPULT

Your sugar cubes will do a little dance through the air as
they soar toward your edible walls and towers!

MATERIALS

1 wooden clothespin
6 x 6 in. piece cardboard
Hot glue gun*
2 corks
1 large craft stick
1 large box sugar cubes
Water bottle cap

STEAM CONNECTION

This catapult is perfect for physics fans! Catapults involve potential and kinetic energy in action. When the craft stick and clothespin are pulled back, they have potential energy (energy stored in an object as a result of its position, such as a wrecking ball about to swing). As the springs in the clothespin are released, it transfers kinetic energy (energy of an object in motion) to the sugar cube, which is what sends the cube soaring. Switch the sugar cube out with a different object and see if it breaks down your wall more—or less—effectively!

1 With <u>adult supervision</u>, hot glue the clothespin to the cardboard.

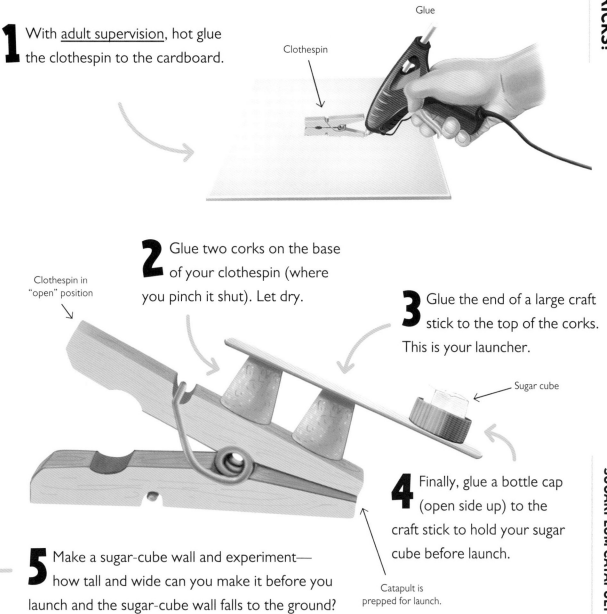

Glue

Clothespin

2 Glue two corks on the base of your clothespin (where you pinch it shut). Let dry.

Clothespin in "open" position

3 Glue the end of a large craft stick to the top of the corks. This is your launcher.

Sugar cube

4 Finally, glue a bottle cap (open side up) to the craft stick to hold your sugar cube before launch.

5 Make a sugar-cube wall and experiment—how tall and wide can you make it before you launch and the sugar-cube wall falls to the ground?

Catapult is prepped for launch.

CANDY CANE CAPER

Your elf won't be able to resist a taste of the candy cane, only
to get caught by this nifty pulley contraption!

DIFFICULTY

ELF APPEAL

MATERIALS

Small pulley purchased from local hardware
    store
Plastic milk crate
Thick string or zip tie
String
Craft glue
Paper cup
1 piece cardboard, at least 24 x 24 in.
Christmas decorations
Plastic snow
Tape (optional)

STEAM CONNECTION

A pulley is a simple machine composed of a small
wheel with a grooved rim fitted to a rope or chain
used to pull heavy loads. A pulley makes lifting
a load (in this case the Styrofoam cup) easier
because it changes the direction of the pulling
force. Pulling down on a rope going through a
pulley allows you to work *with* gravity to move a
load *against* gravity. The more you wrap the rope
around a pulley wheel, or the more wheels you
have, the easier it is to lift the load.

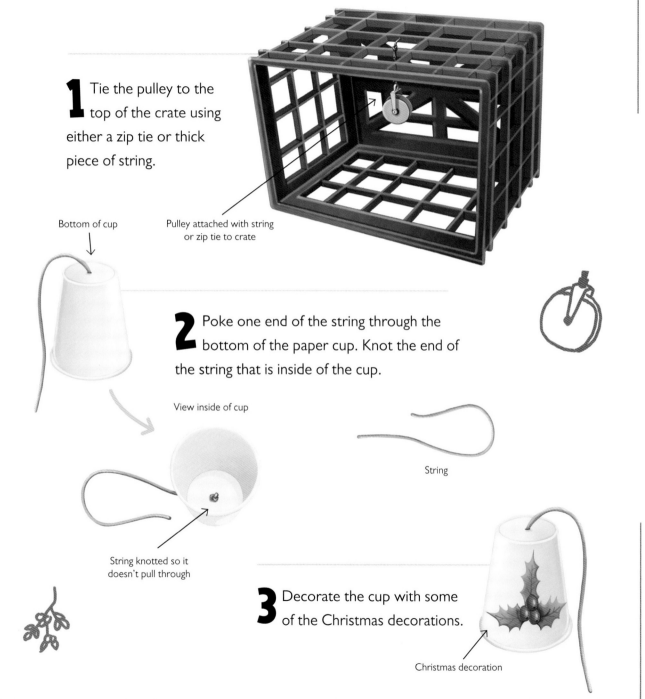

1 Tie the pulley to the top of the crate using either a zip tie or thick piece of string.

Bottom of cup

Pulley attached with string or zip tie to crate

2 Poke one end of the string through the bottom of the paper cup. Knot the end of the string that is inside of the cup.

View inside of cup

String

String knotted so it doesn't pull through

3 Decorate the cup with some of the Christmas decorations.

Christmas decoration

4 Tape a sturdy piece of cardboard along the bottom of your crate to ensure the elf won't fall through the hole and escape.

Candy cane securing paper clip

Piece of cardboard

5 Take your string with the attached cup and wrap it around the groove in the pulley wheel. Secure the free end of the string to a paper clip. Using a candy cane, weigh the string and paper clip down to temporarily hold it in place.

Note: This string should be taut, and the paper clip and candy cane should be directly under the cup.

6 Decorate crate with tinsel, garland, ornaments, or other decorations. When the elf sees the candy cane, he'll pick it up and the cup will catch him!

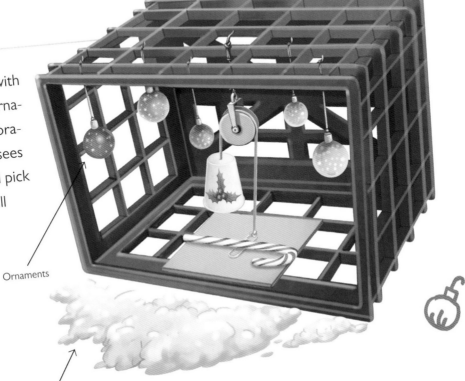

Ornaments

Fake snow

DID YOU KNOW?

Mistletoe is traditionally associated with the snowy weather of the winter holidays, but it actually grows in various climates all over the world, including the deserts of the American Southwest.

CRYSTAL SNOWFLAKE ORNAMENTS

Create your very own snowflake that you can hang up on a Christmas tree!

DIFFICULTY

ELF APPEAL

MATERIALS

Pipe cleaners

Scissors*

String

Pencil

Jar

2 cups boiling water*

6 tablespoons Borax Laundry Booster

(Caution: Do not ingest.)

Holiday ribbon

STEAM CONNECTION

Borax has special symmetrical *molecules*, the microscopic particles that make up a substance. When Borax is added to boiling water, its molecules dissolve due to the high temperature, but as the solution cools, the Borax molecules begin to expand and attach themselves to the inserted pipe cleaner, forming crystals.

1 With <u>adult supervision</u>, cut pipe cleaners into various sizes of strips and twist together to create a snowflake shape.

Pipe cleaners

2 Tie string around the top of the snowflake tip and fasten the other end around the middle of a pencil. Place snowflake in jar with pencil resting across the top.

Tip: Make sure the pipe cleaners do not touch the sides of the glass!

String

Pencil

3 With <u>adult supervision</u>, dissolve Borax into boiling water and pour into jar.

4 Let snowflake sit in the solution for twenty-four hours. Keep checking back to watch the crystals form!

5 Once set, remove the snowflake from the jar and let dry. Then, tie a ribbon to the snowflake to create a snowflake ornament.

REINDEER LIGHTS AWAY!

Santa's reindeer leader will pique your elf's curiosity as he tiptoes near this glowing trap!

DIFFICULTY

ELF APPEAL

MATERIALS

Reindeer template (page 45 and 46)

Scissors*

Construction paper, various colors

Markers or crayons

1 small LED light

1 small, flat lithium battery*

Electrical tape

1 empty cereal box

Glue

Tape

Wrapping paper

Ribbons

Building blocks

Velcro or putty to attach reindeer inside box
(optional)

Soft scarf, sock, or tissues to cushion your
elf's fall (optional)

STEAM CONNECTION

This trap uses electricity through LED lights to draw elves in. *LED* is short for "light emitting diode." These small light bulbs produce a lot of light for their size; when turned on, the energy from the battery or the electrical circuit causes the electrons within the light bulb to speed up. The electrons release extra energy and create *photons*—and you get light!

Reindeer template

1 To make the reindeer head, cut out the template and trace onto a sheet of brown construction paper. Cut out the reindeer from the construction paper and have a parent punch a small hole near the center to insert the LED light for the nose.

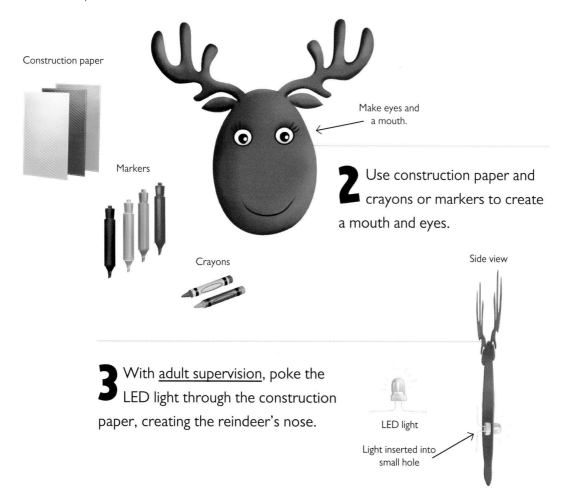

Construction paper

Make eyes and a mouth.

Markers

2 Use construction paper and crayons or markers to create a mouth and eyes.

Crayons

Side view

3 With <u>adult supervision</u>, poke the LED light through the construction paper, creating the reindeer's nose.

LED light

Light inserted into small hole

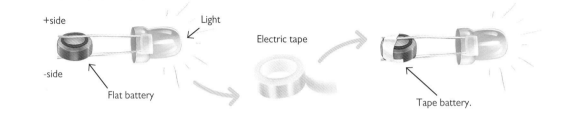

+side
Light
-side
Flat battery
Electric tape
Tape battery.

4 On the back of the reindeer's head, use <u>adult supervision</u> to bend the terminals of the LED light to lie flat on each side of the battery. Make sure the positive side of the battery is touching the positive terminal, and the negative side is touching only the negative terminal. The positive terminal peg will be slightly longer than the negative end.

DID YOU KNOW?

Adult reindeer have a special tissue in the nasal cavity called *nasal mucosa*, which is rich in red blood cells and helps protect against cold weather. This tissue can also cause their noses to become RED!

5 Use electric tape to tape down the terminal and battery for long-lasting glow.

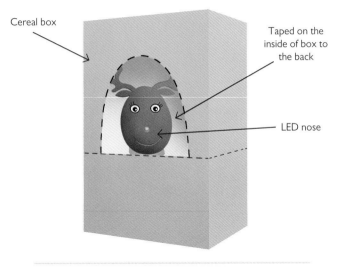

Cereal box
Taped on the inside of box to the back
LED nose

6 Cut out an arch on the top half of a cereal box. Tape your reindeer to the back of the box (the opposite side from the archway), glowing nose facing out.

Tip: Use putty or Velcro strips on the back of your reindeer so you can change the position of it, if necessary.

Add decorations to box.

7 Decorate your box with wrapping paper and ribbons. Trim the archway for an extra-special touch and place something soft on the bottom of the box—we don't want our sweet elf to get hurt!

Small ornaments, candy canes, ribbons

Wrapping paper

Tape

8 Use building blocks to make stairs that lead up to the cereal opening. Your elf will not be able to resist Rudolph's bright light, only to have a (soft) landing into your box!

Building block stairs

49

SANTA'S REINDEER TEAM RACE

Who can deliver presents the fastest? This physics activity will have you cheering as you root for your reindeer to cross the finish line!

DIFFICULTY

ELF APPEAL

MATERIALS

String, several spools

Straight straws

Package of balloons

Tape

Decorations for reindeer's face: googly eyes, pom-poms, etc.

Markers

Ending points for your racetrack

(2 chairs will do.)

STEAM CONNECTION

This fun and simple reindeer race involves the physics of action and reaction! Air escaping = balloon propulsion! When you blow up the balloon, you are filling it with air that is pressurized. As you launch the balloon to race, the air is released backward, thrusting the balloon forward.

1 Set up your racetrack. Cut two pieces of string, each at least 8–12 ft. long. Thread each piece of string through one straw (this is what the reindeer flies down on).

Straw

Strings tied
to chair

2 Tape the two pieces of string, parallel to each other, to the ending points of the race-track. Make sure the string is taut before you tape it down.

3 Blow up balloons, and clamp the end while you decorate. Adorn the balloons with reindeer faces made with markers, googly eyes, and pom-poms.

4 Prepare for takeoff! Wrap a piece of tape around the racetrack straws with the sticky side up—you are making one loop of tape around the straw. Repeat this step for each string and straw.

Note: The pieces of tape cannot touch the actual string, or your reindeer cannot zoom down the track!

5 Place your reindeer balloons on the sticky side of the tape so they will not fall off the straw as they fly down the string racetrack!

6 Once you are ready to let them go, unclamp the balloon openings and watch them race!

Not the winner? Blow the balloons back up for more racing fun!

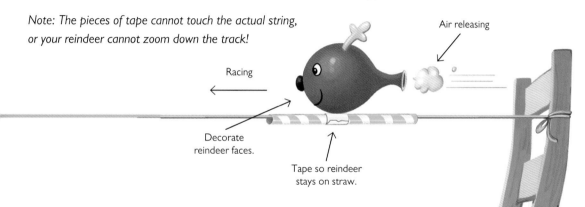

Air releasing

Racing

Decorate
reindeer faces.

Tape so reindeer
stays on straw.

PINE TREE PITFALL

Elves will love getting in touch with their outdoor selves as they are lured into a little tree house—only to fall in!

DIFFICULTY

ELF APPEAL

MATERIALS

Foam board (8½ x 11 in. or larger)

Wrapping paper

Tape

Foam cylinder, at least 3 in. in diameter or more and approximately 8+ in. high, preferably hollow

Crafting knife*

Ice cream scoop or large spoon

Brown paint

Paintbrush

Hot glue gun*

15–20 large craft sticks

Tinsel

Putty

White index card for sign

STEAM CONNECTION

This trap has a spiral staircase that will carry the elf up to the top of the trap. A spiral is a shape or pattern that winds in a continuous curve, gradually widening (or tightening) around a central point. Spirals can be seen all over in nature—this pattern is found not only on plants and animals, but also in galaxies and weather patterns.

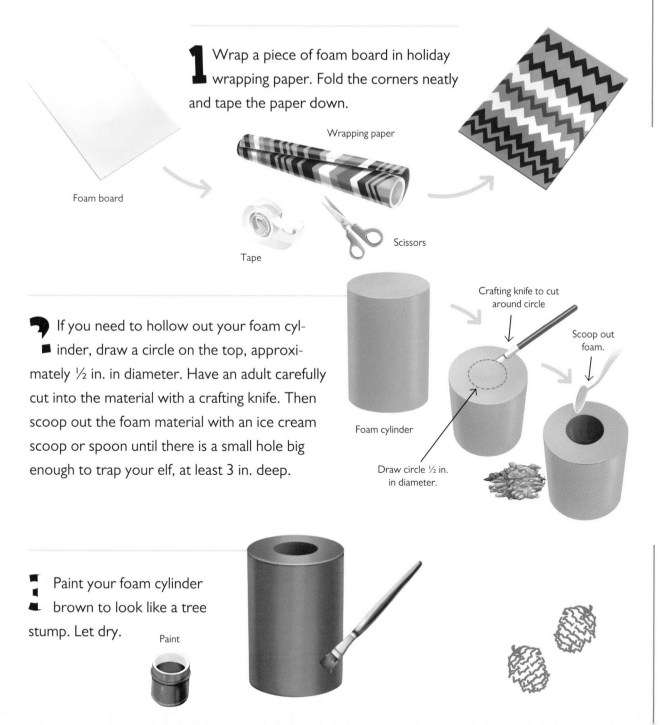

1 Wrap a piece of foam board in holiday wrapping paper. Fold the corners neatly and tape the paper down.

Wrapping paper

Foam board

Tape

Scissors

2 If you need to hollow out your foam cylinder, draw a circle on the top, approximately ½ in. in diameter. Have an adult carefully cut into the material with a crafting knife. Then scoop out the foam material with an ice cream scoop or spoon until there is a small hole big enough to trap your elf, at least 3 in. deep.

Foam cylinder

Crafting knife to cut around circle

Scoop out foam.

Draw circle ½ in. in diameter.

3 Paint your foam cylinder brown to look like a tree stump. Let dry.

Paint

Hot glue base to board.

4 With <u>adult supervision</u>, hot glue your hollow tree stump to the foam board.

Insert craft sticks into foam to create spiral staircase.

5 Insert large craft sticks into the tree stump in an ascending spiral to create stairs, leaving approximately 2 in. of the craft stick out for each step.

Tip: Prior to poking the sticks in, make little marks to ensure proper placement.

DID YOU KNOW?

Evergreen trees have been used by cultures throughout the world to celebrate the winter season for thousands of years. Ancient Romans and Druidic Celts alike decorated their homes and temples with evergreen boughs as a symbol of life and renewal. Decorated indoor Christmas trees is a tradition believed to have begun in 16th century Germany, and was brought to the United States by Christian German settlers in Pennsylvania, but the custom didn't become popular until the late 19th century. Now in just the United States alone, approximately 350 million Christmas trees are grown each year.

6 Fill the hole of the tree stump with tinsel.

7 Using the index card, create a sign that will draw your elf in: "Rest Stop" or "Free Candy Canes Inside," for example. Glue the sign to a craft stick and then use putty to stick the sign onto the foam board. Your elf will think this is a snuggly, sparkly pillow until he falls inside!

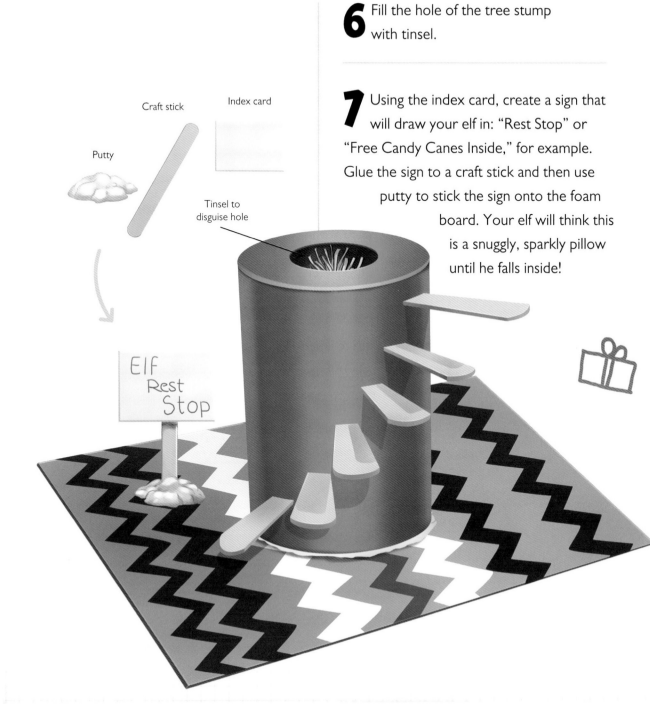

Craft stick

Index card

Putty

Tinsel to disguise hole

Elf Rest Stop

TINKER TREES

Create mini trees with a fun, new twist and use them to decorate any trap or room!

STEAM CONNECTION

Engineers, carpenters, and other builders use these fasteners to connect two or more objects together and to strengthen a hold between objects. We're bringing an artistic flair to this project by using these materials to create trees! Experiment with different size bolts, nuts, and washers and see how many different tree combinations you can make!

MATERIALS

⅝ in. diameter bolts in various lengths (one per tree)

⅝ in. nuts (one per tree)

Washers ranging from small to large in diameter

1 Place one of the bolts vertically on a flat surface to create the base of the tree trunk.

2 Twist on a nut that rests slightly above the end of the bolt and add a large washer. Continue adding nuts and washers all the way up the bolt and end with a nut to hold the top in place. To make your creation look like a Christmas tree, make sure the washers go from large to small!

3 Create a metallic Christmas tree farm with your holiday hardware. Use the trees to decorate any trap!

Washer

Nut

Bolt

SANTA'S SODA BOTTLE

Our elf will swirl down this soda bottle in no time as he hopes
to snag some new stockings and a sweet drink.

DIFFICULTY

ELF APPEAL

MATERIALS

Large plastic soda bottle, empty and cleaned

Sharp scissors/knife*

Paint, various colors

Paintbrush

Ribbon

Hot glue gun*

Cotton balls (optional)

Tinsel (optional)

Red felt

1 package straws

Putty or tape

White index card

STEAM CONNECTION

Once the elf steps into the funnel, gravity will
spiral him into the second part of the trap. You
can test out your funnel by tossing a coin in. Due
to the funnel's curves and downhill shape, the
coin will keep descending down the funnel vortex.
However, if your coin is going too fast, it will
remain on the rim of your funnel/inverted bottle
top; if it is too slow, it will quickly go toward the
center hole! The shape of your funnel determines
the object's direction, speed, and ultimate descent
into your trap!

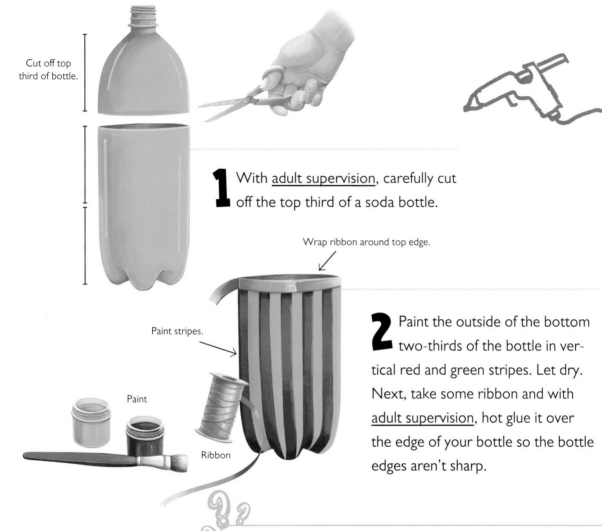

Cut off top third of bottle.

1 With <u>adult supervision</u>, carefully cut off the top third of a soda bottle.

Wrap ribbon around top edge.

Paint stripes.

Paint

Ribbon

2 Paint the outside of the bottom two-thirds of the bottle in vertical red and green stripes. Let dry. Next, take some ribbon and with <u>adult supervision</u>, hot glue it over the edge of your bottle so the bottle edges aren't sharp.

DID YOU KNOW?

In 2008, residents of Bethel, Maine built the tallest snowman—or in this case, snowwoman—in the world! At the height of 112 ft., the snowwoman was just a few feet shorter than the Statue of Liberty. Thirteen million pounds of snow, eight pairs of skis, three truck tires, and two spruce trees came together to create this incredible snowwoman!

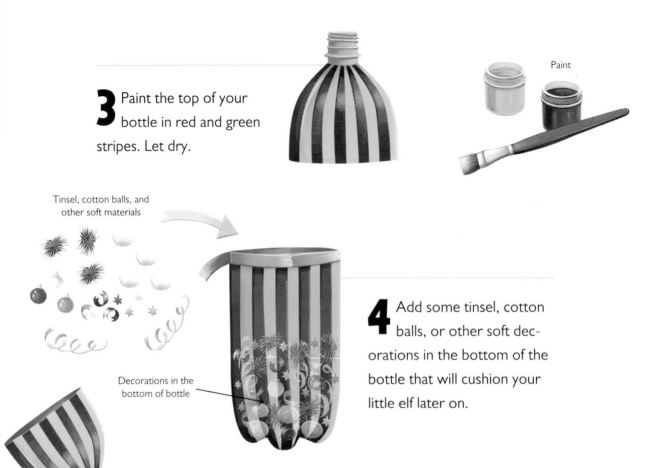

3 Paint the top of your bottle in red and green stripes. Let dry.

Paint

Tinsel, cotton balls, and other soft materials

Decorations in the bottom of bottle

4 Add some tinsel, cotton balls, or other soft decorations in the bottom of the bottle that will cushion your little elf later on.

Add top to the inside.

5 Turn the bottle top upside down and insert it into the bottom section of the bottle, like a funnel.

Hot glue ribbon around bottle edge.

6 With <u>adult supervision</u>, hot glue another piece of ribbon around the diameter to secure the two pieces in place.

Glue all around rim.

7 Cut out six to ten mini stockings out of red felt and, with <u>adult supervision</u>, hot glue them around the rim of the bottle.

Felt

Felt stocking

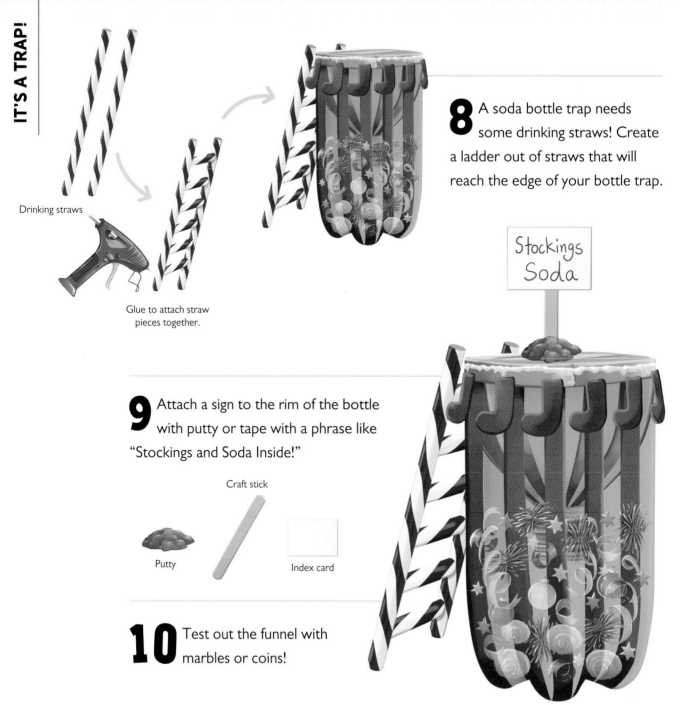

Drinking straws

Glue to attach straw pieces together.

8 A soda bottle trap needs some drinking straws! Create a ladder out of straws that will reach the edge of your bottle trap.

Stockings Soda

9 Attach a sign to the rim of the bottle with putty or tape with a phrase like "Stockings and Soda Inside!"

Craft stick

Putty

Index card

10 Test out the funnel with marbles or coins!

JINGLE BELL ROCK

Watch your bells dance to Christmas carols in this easy and fun science project!

DIFFICULTY

ELF APPEAL

MATERIALS

Medium- to large-size mason jar
Clear carbonated beverage
Bag of tiny bells

Mason jar

1 Fill jar with carbonated beverage.

2 Drop six to eight bells in.

3 Watch them dance!

STEAM CONNECTION

The principles of *density* and *buoyancy* are front and center in this activity! When you initially drop your bells in, they sink to the bottom because they have more *mass* than the liquid. But the tiny air bubbles from the carbonation cause the bells to float up through the glass because the bubbles act as tiny life vests and make the bells more buoyant. Air bubbles popping means the bells sink down again.

Clear carbonated drink

Bubbles

Jingle bells

DOWN THE CHIMNEY

Elves will love taking a ride down this marble-run-style
chimney, only to land in a handwoven basket.

DIFFICULTY

ELF APPEAL

MATERIALS

5 paper-towel tubes

Brown paint

Gold paint (optional)

Sponge

Paintbrush

Scissors*

1 large piece cardboard

1 package pipe cleaners

Tape

Deep container (optional)

Marble (optional)

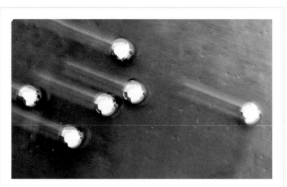

STEAM CONNECTION

This trap uses a marble run and shows physics
at its finest! Marble runs demonstrate the
conservation of energy, including acceleration
and gravity. When a marble (or, in this case, the
elf!) is resting, it has stored-up energy, known as
potential energy. Once the marble takes off down
the tubes, that energy is converted into energy of
motion (known as kinetic energy) and combines
with gravity to pull the marble downward.
Alternating the positions of your tubes will change
the marble speed, so experiment with different
angles to find out the quickest way to get your elf
to the bottom of the trap!

1 Use the sponge and brown paint to create a brick pattern on three paper-towel tubes.

Paint

Paper-towel tubes

Sponges

2 Cut the two remaining tubes in half lengthwise to make some slides. You will only use three of the slides. Paint them brown or gold. Let dry.

Three painted tube slides

Tubes cut in half

Paint

DID YOU KNOW?

||||||||||||||||||||||||||||||||||||||||||||||||||||

Hanging stockings by the fire dates back to a Dutch tradition of leaving shoes full of food for St. Nicholas's donkeys!

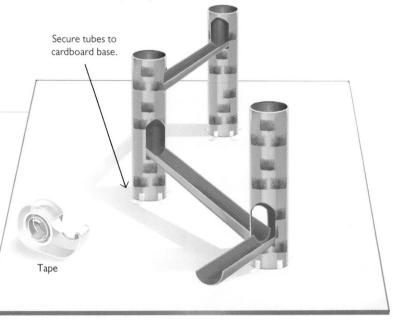

3 Take one of the paper-towel tubes from step 1 and cut a hole near the top. For the second paper-towel tube from step 1, cut two holes near the middle. For the third paper-towel tube from step 1, cut two holes near the bottom. Make sure the holes are big enough for the "slides" to rest in. We are creating three towers with three slides—the last slide will release the elf into the basket. Depending on how you engineer this trap, the last slide might need to be shortened in order for it to reach the basket.

Tip: Once your chutes are dry, and before you tape anything down, experiment with your slide arrangement! Stagger the tubes so that higher cutouts/slide openings flow into the lower cutouts/slide openings.

Holes for the slides

Secure tubes to cardboard base.

4 Tape down your towers on top of your cardboard and prop your slides in the cutouts from step 3. Test it out with a marble!

Tape

Pipe cleaners

5 Twist together pipe cleaners to create a ladder and prop up against the starting tower.

Tie to create ladder.

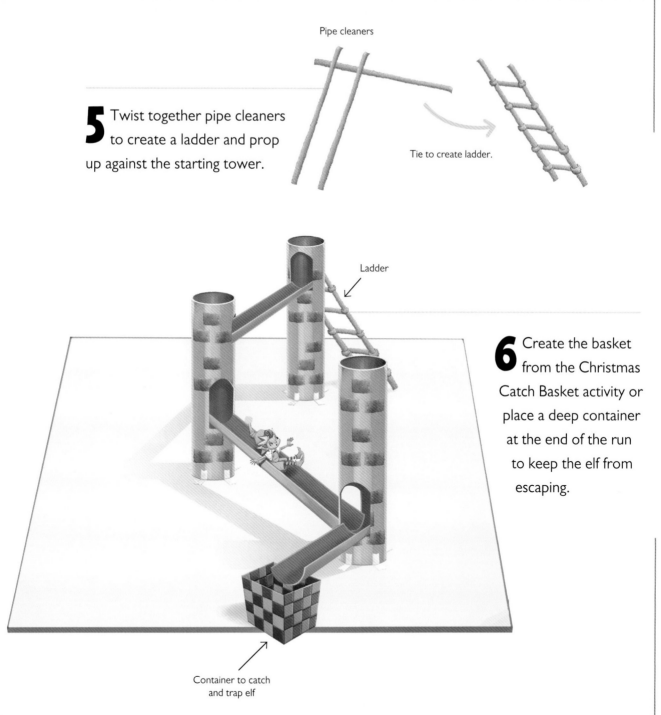

Ladder

6 Create the basket from the Christmas Catch Basket activity or place a deep container at the end of the run to keep the elf from escaping.

Container to catch and trap elf

CHRISTMAS CATCH BASKET

Get in touch with your artistic skills to weave a perfect little nesting spot for your elf! Add this basket to Down the Chimney or other traps!

DIFFICULTY

ELF APPEAL

MATERIALS

3 pieces construction paper, 9 x 12 in.,
    various colors
Ruler
Scissors or paper cutter*
Glue

STEAM CONNECTION

The art of weaving dates back to Neolithic times—approximately 12,000 years ago! This technique was used to entwine branches and twigs to create baskets and various types of shelters. Weaving was also used to create clothes—a practice that still continues today. Different threads or yarn are intertwined to create fabric. Weavers usually work on a special apparatus called a *loom*.

In this activity, we'll be using the terms *warp* and *weft* to refer to the threads being woven. Warp threads are threads that stay stationary during the creation process, and the weft threads are the ones woven over and under the warp threads.

1 Cut four 9 x ½ in. strips of the first piece of construction paper and set aside for step 9.

9 in.

2 Cut four 10 x ½ in. strips of the second piece of construction paper and set aside for step 5.

10 in.

3 Cut four 10 x ½ in. strips of the third piece of construction paper.

10 in.

4 Place the 10 in. strips of paper from step 3 side by side vertically. These are your warp threads.

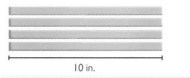

5 Lay the other 10 in. pieces from step 2 horizontally next to the four strips from step 4. These are your weft threads. Weave the weft threads over and under the warp threads, creating a square. This is the base of the basket.

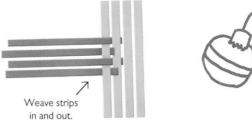

Weave strips in and out.

6 Adjust the paper to create a 2 in. square from the woven strips. Each unwoven edge should measure 4 in. long.

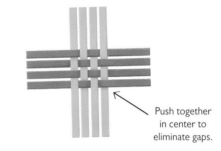

Push together in center to eliminate gaps.

7 Glue down each corner of the woven square to keep it secure.

Fold up sides to create the basket.

8 Fold the unwoven, 4 in. ends toward the inner square. These will become the sides of the basket.

9 Take the 9 in. strips from step 1 and use a ruler to mark every 2 in. on the strips (the last section of the strip will have an additional inch). Fold the strips on each 2 in. mark to create a square and glue the ends together, using the additional inch to connect the sides. Repeat with the three remaining strips.

Make four squares with 9 in. strips.

Glue overlapping edges together to close square.

2 in.

2 in.

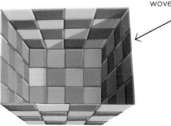

Squares from step 9 woven into basket

10 Weave a square from step 9 through the basket's side strips— over and under alternating pieces. Repeat with the remaining three squares as you build up the sides. Your basket should only be 2 in. high.

11 Fold the extra 2 in. of paper at the top inside of the basket and glue down to keep secure.

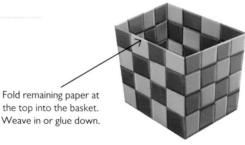

Fold remaining paper at the top into the basket. Weave in or glue down.

SANTA'S SLEIGH RIDE

Uh oh! Santa's sleigh has turned upside down and scattered the presents all over! Your concerned little elf will need to investigate until the sleigh falls down and traps him inside!

DIFFICULTY

ELF APPEAL

MATERIALS

Sleigh template (page 73 and 74)
24 x 36 in. foam board
Pencil or marker
Construction paper
Red paint
Paintbrush
Crafting knife*
Screwdriver
Hot glue gun*
Shoebox or similar style box (top not necessary)
Holiday stickers or gemstone stickers
Scissors*
String
Tape

STEAM CONNECTION

Gravity plays a crucial role in this trap! Gravity is the force that keeps objects (including people) grounded on Earth. It's because of gravitational force that a ripe apple will fall to the ground instead of floating away into outer space! In this trap, the weight of the presents on the string is strong enough to hold the sleigh into place, but once your elf grabs the presents, gravity will pull the sleigh down and capture the elf!

1 Cut out the sleigh template on pages 73-74. Cut out the individual sleigh pieces.

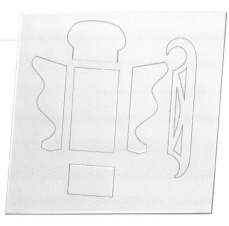

Scissors

Sleigh template

Tape down the sleigh cutouts.

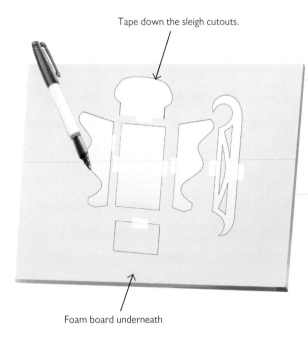

Foam board underneath

2 Tape the sleigh cutouts onto the foam board to keep them in place.

3 Trace the pieces onto the foam board using a marker or pencil. Make sure to trace the rail twice! Once you've traced the cutouts, remove them from the foam board.

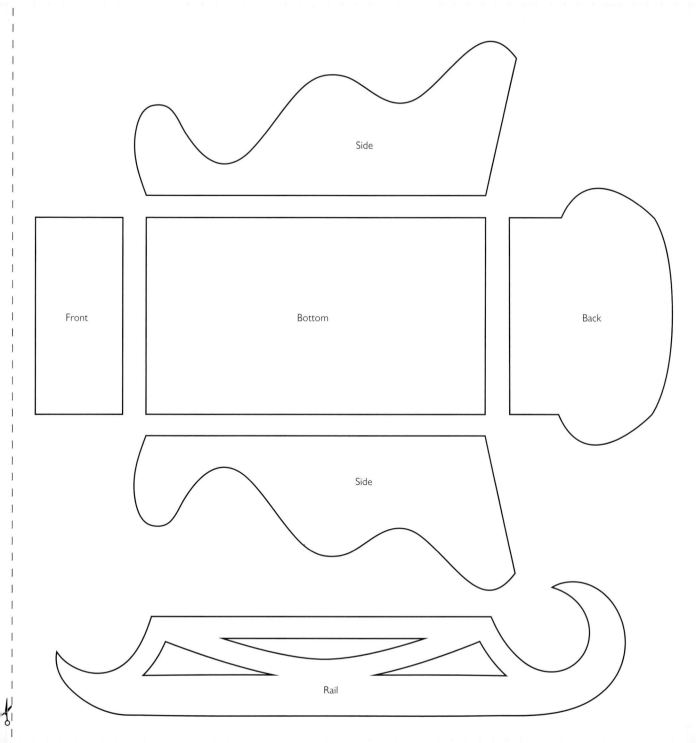

Side

Front

Bottom

Back

Side

Rail

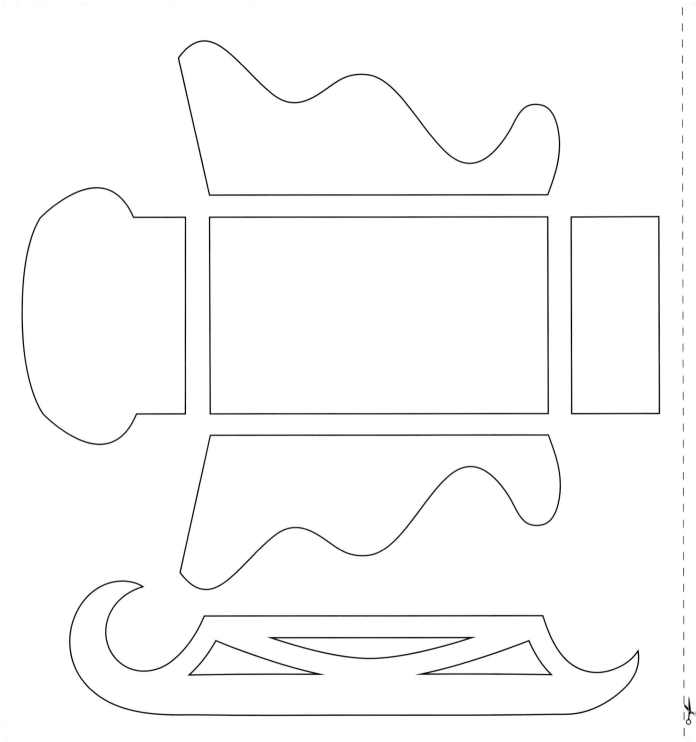

4 Ask an adult to use a craft knife to cut out the sleigh pieces from the foam board.

Pieces popped out of board

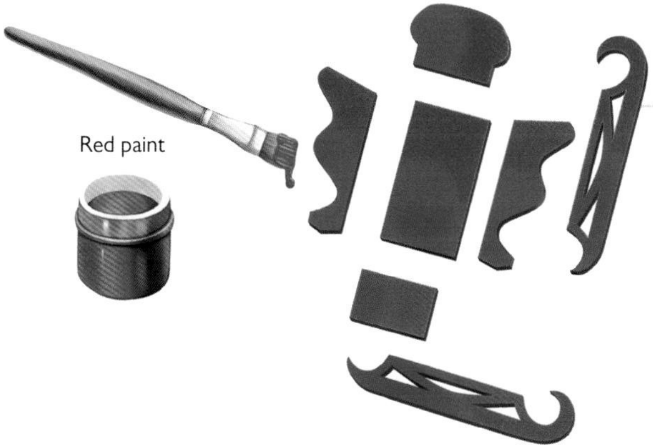

Red paint

5 Paint the sleigh pieces red.

6 With <u>adult supervision</u>, use a screw-driver to poke a small hole through the center of the bottom sleigh piece.

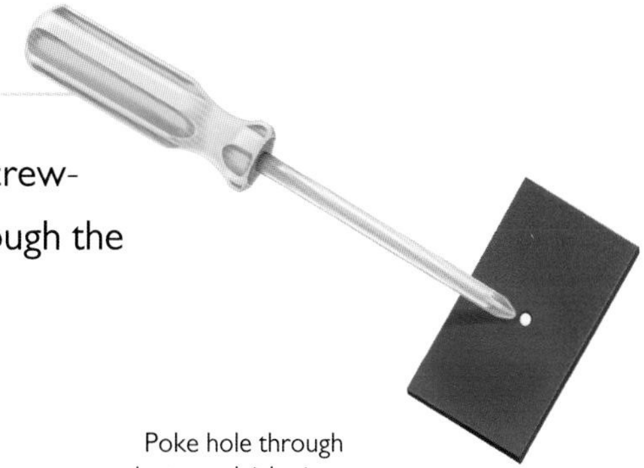

Poke hole through bottom sleigh piece.

7 With <u>adult supervision</u>, use a hot glue gun to assemble your sleigh, carefully applying glue along the edges of the sleigh pieces. Let dry.

Hot glue along edges.

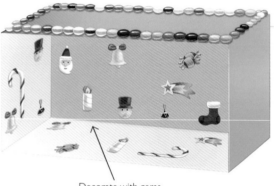

Decorate with gems and stickers.

8 Decorate the box with holiday or gemstone stickers.

Top of box

Back of box

9 At the top of your box, poke a hole directly in the center—this is where your sleigh will hang from. Poke another hole at the center of the back of the box, still in line with the top hole.

Centered

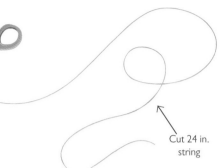

Yarn or string

10 With <u>adult supervision</u>, cut a 24 in. piece of string.

Cut 24 in. string

11 Pull the string through the hole on the sleigh and tie a knot on the bottom of it so the string cannot pull through.

Bottom of sleigh

Knot so string won't pull through when sleigh is upside down

DID YOU KNOW?

If each of the children on the planet (approximately 2.5 billion people) got a toy weighing 7 ounces, Santa's sleigh would be transporting 500,000 tons of toys!

12 Thread the remainder of the string through the hole at the top of your box, then into the box through the back centered hole. Temporarily tape the string down directly beneath the sleigh to keep the sleigh dangling.

The string should be taut, so when it is released, the sleigh falls down. If the string gets snagged on the edges of the holes, you can cover the edges with tape so the string can pass smoothly.

13 Create little paper gift boxes with your construction paper by cutting a 3 in. square out of paper. Next, cut 1 in. squares from each corner so the paper resembles a plus sign. Then, fold the edges into a box and secure with tape. Fill the box with little candies or other gifts.

Depending on the thickness of the foam board, you may need multiple boxes to hold the sleigh up.

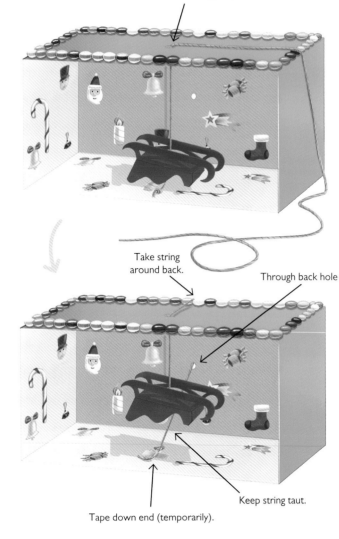

Thread through top.

Take string around back.

Through back hole

Keep string taut.

Tape down end (temporarily).

3 in.

3 in.

Cut out 1 in. squares to create a + sign.

Open top

Fold up sides.

Tape

14 Untape the string from the bottom of the box and place the presents directly under your sleigh, on top of the string. Your elf won't be able to resist a peek! Once he lifts up the presents—snap! The string will release and the elf will be under Santa's sleigh!

Presents on top of string

PARACHUTING ELVES

Geronimo! This clever parachute is perfect for elves hopping down from Santa's sleigh!

DIFFICULTY

ELF APPEAL

MATERIALS

Small paper cup
Screwdriver
Plastic grocery bag
Scissors*
String
Small plastic elf or modeling clay
Tape measure

STEAM CONNECTION

Gravity and air resistance are at play in this fun parachute activity! Air resistance is a type of force that is caused by air and works against an object moving through the air. Opening the parachute greatly increases this resistance and therefore makes the parachute descend more slowly. You can try several different experiments, switching out a coffee filter or plastic baggie for the parachute, a different size cup, or even different length string for your parachute. The fun of this project is that it is quick to assemble and reassemble with alternate materials. What about the weight of your clay elf? Can you take different durable Christmas figurines and time their landing?

1 Use the screwdriver to poke four holes under the rim of the cup (where you sip). They should be equal distance apart.

2 Flatten the bag and measure a 14 in. square. With <u>adult supervision,</u> carefully cut a square out of the bag.

3 Cut four pieces of string, 14 in. in length. Pinch a corner of the plastic bag and tie one end of string around it. Repeat for each string and corner of your parachute.

4 Feed the ends of your four strings from step 3 into the four holes of your cup (four strings tied to four holes) and tie a knot so the strings don't come through the hole. Keep the strings the same length so your parachute does not descend lopsided!

5 Create a small elf from modeling clay, or use the elf from Mistletoe Mischief or another elf figurine.

6 Test it out with your elf or other Christmas character. Carefully place them in the cup and time how long it takes them to reach the ground from various dropoff points.

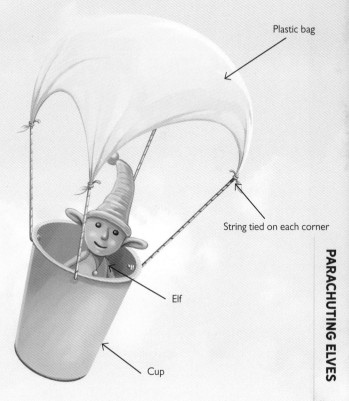

Plastic bag

String tied on each corner

Elf

Cup

MAKE YOUR OWN ELF-TRAPPING KIT

Put your own creative skills to the test and create your very own elf trap!

DIFFICULTY

ELF APPEAL

USE YOUR IMAGINATION!

Implement ideas from the traps described in this book and create your own!

SUGGESTED MATERIALS

How to Catch an Elf by Adam Wallace

Pencil and notepad

Construction paper

Glue and tape

Cardboard boxes, various sizes

Paint and paintbrush

String

Paper-towel tubes

Craft sticks

Twist ties

Mini cups

Candy canes

Gumdrops

Tinsel

Ornament hooks

Wrapping paper

Basket for all your materials

1

2

3

4

_____

_____

_____

_____

_____

5

_____

_____

_____

_____

_____

6

_____

_____

_____

_____

_____

7

_____

_____

_____

_____

ABOUT THE AUTHOR

|||||||||||||||||||||||||||||||||||||||||||||||||||||||||||||||||||||||||||||||||||||||||||||||||||||||||||||||

Larissa Juliano lives in upstate New York with her husband and three young children. She is an elementary teacher and children's book writer who is passionate about sharing literature to inspire children's creativity. You can check out her other books on her website larissajuliano.com.